Dwayne's Guitar Lessons presents:

Electric Guitar

101

By

Guitar Teacher
DwayneJenkins

Tritone publishing © 2025

Introduction

The electric guitar was invented out of necessity. It was invented because the acoustic guitar could not be heard when playing with other instruments in an ensemble.

To make the guitar louder, it needed to be redesigned and amplified. Hence, the electric guitar. Since doing so, the electric guitar has become one of the most popular instruments on the planet.

But when it comes to learning to play the instrument, it can be a bit overwhelming at first. Thre are a lot more things to deal with than there are learning to play the acoustic. Especially when you add the amplifier.

That is why Electric Guitar 101 was created. To make it easier to learn, thus making it fun to play. This method book goes through a simple step-by-step system of lessons that anyone can learn from.

With full-color pictures, diagrams, and notation that take out the guesswork. All you need to do is take it one lesson at a time and you will be on your way.

You will start by learning about the guitar itself. All the parts of the guitar and how it is different from the acoustic. You will then proceed with learning about what each hand does to play the guitar.

Introduction

You will then look at how to tune the guitar and what device is best to make this happen. What the names of the strings are so that you know what to tune them to. You will learn the importance and benefits of using a guitar pick.

You'll then learn about the guitar amplifier and what cool things you can do with it. How you can use it to not only control the volume but also to shape your overall guitar tone.

You will learn about chords and reading chord charts. With diagrams, you'll be able to learn them quickly. Then you'll learn how to create rhythms to make them sound like music.

You'll also learn some tips on how to play lead guitar, basic music theory, practice habits, and ear training. All in an easy method that takes out all the confusion.

Yep, it's all right here in Electric Guitar 101. An easy-to-understand guidebook that will have you playing guitar in no time. Just follow it step by step, and with a little daily practice, you'll be having fun in no time. Best of luck.

Dwayne Jenkins 3/2025

Tritone Publishing © 2025

Contents

Tritone Publishing © 2025

Contents

continued

Tritone Publishing © 2025

Chapter 1

Getting Started

Lesson 1: Electric guitar anatomy

Welcome to Electric Guitar 101. This will be a brief course to get you started quickly and easily. When it comes to learning an instrument, the electric guitar is a great place to start. It's very popular, fun to play, and readily available at a reasonable price.

So, like any good craftsman, we want to make sure we know our tools of the trade. In our case, it is the electric guitar. Let's take a look at what it's all about.

Electric guitar anatomy:

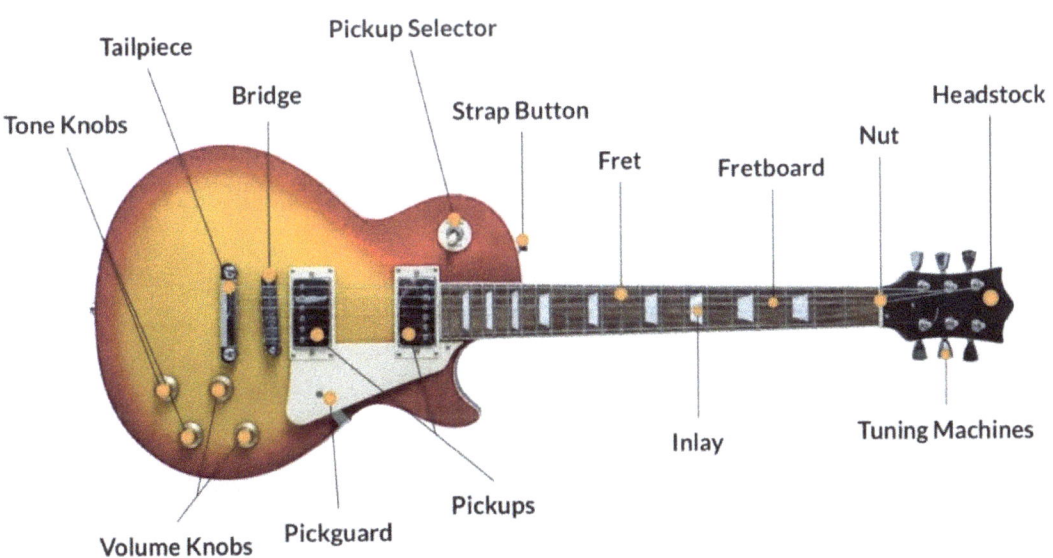

Headstock: An area for the tuners that holds on the strings.

Tuners: These allow you to adjust the string's tension to a certain pitch.

Nut: A slot that the strings go through and stay separated.

Neck: Holds the nut, fretboard, frets, markers, strings, and head.

Strings: These vibrate at a certain pitch and create sound.

Frets: These allow you to quickly change the pitch of the strings.

Fret markers: These determine where you are along the fretboard.

Body: This attaches the strings to the bridge across the pickups.

Pickups: These pick up the string vibration to create sound.

Bridge: Anchors the strings to the guitar body.

Tone knobs: These allow you to control the volume & tone.

Study the diagram and get familiar with the guitar. Since you're going to be spending time learning to make beautiful music with it, you'll need to get to know it. The better you know it, the better guitar player you will become.

Lesson 2: Holding the guitar

Now that we've been introduced to the electric guitar, we can look into how to hold it. When playing the guitar, we can play it either sitting down or standing up. I recommend for our purpose here today, we learn it sitting down. It will be much easier.

The main thing we want to do is make sure that the guitar is comfortably in our hands. We can reach the fretboard easily, and we can reach our arm around the body to strum chords and pick strings.

Your fretboard hand will be used to form chords, and your picking hand will be used to create rhythm.

As you can see from the two pictures above, the guitar is being played in both positions Either way, we want to make sure that we're comfortable and can access everything.

Tritone Publishing © 2025

Now that we know how to hold the guitar, let's examine how each hand should be positioned when creating music out of the instrument.

Both hands should be relaxed and able to reach all parts of the guitar that are necessary to play it.

The fretboard hand:

As you can see from the picture to the left, the fretboard hand is the one that forms the chords among multiple strings. So you want your fingers to be able to reach firmly around the fretboard with your thumb in the back.

The picking hand:

In the picture to the right, you can see how the picking hand is positioned. The arm is stretched around the front with the pick is held in place. Your hand should be relaxed and able to move freely across all six strings.

When playing the guitar, you want to make sure your hands stay relaxed and the guitar is comfortable at all times.

Summary
Chapter 1

In Chapter 1, we have learned some very important aspects. We looked at parts of the electric guitar. This lesson gives us insight into how the guitar works and what makes it tick.

We learned that the electric guitar is different from the acoustic in the fact it has pickups and not a soundhole to pick up the string vibration. Get familiar with your guitar and all the parts that make it what it is.

From the headstock to the tuners, guitar neck, fretboard, fret markers, bridge, and saddle. All these things make up one of the best instruments in the world to play. If you stick with the training, you will see why it has become so popular over the years.

We then learn about how to hold the guitar and what our two hands should be doing. Once we get that guitar in our hands, we begin to make it part of us. We began to make a connection with it. This is our first step into a great new world.

Our fretboard hand will form the chords, and our picking hand will create the rhythm and bring the chords to life. Work on developing these things daily to create wonderful music.

Tritone Publishing © 2025

Chapter 2

Tuning up & Using a pick

Lesson 3: Tuning the guitar

The most important thing about playing the guitar (or any instrument for that matter) is that it must be in tune to sound good. This skill is vital to creating music that sounds pleasant to the ear.

The strings are numbered 1 through 6. You can easily remember this by the thickness of the strings. The biggest string is the highest number, and the thinnest string is the lowest number.

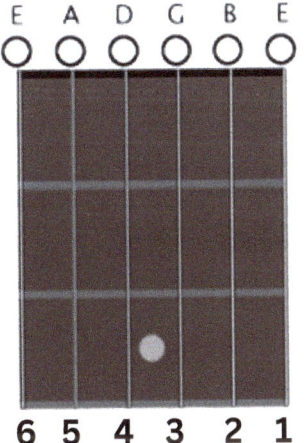

The strings also have names as you can see from the picture. The 6th string is your biggest and is on the left, and the 1st string which is your smallest, is on the right.

So your **6th string is low E, 5th is A, 4th is D, 3rd is G, 2nd is B and your 1st is also E.**

One way to remember the names of the strings is with an acronym like **E**ddie **A**te **D**ynamite **G**ood**B**ye **E**ddie.

Now that we know what the names of the 6 strings are, this is what we will tune them to, and the best way to do that is with an electronic guitar tuner.   There are a few different type, but the most common is the kind that clips on to the guitar headstock.

A clip on tuner   **A clip on tuner attached to the guitar**

   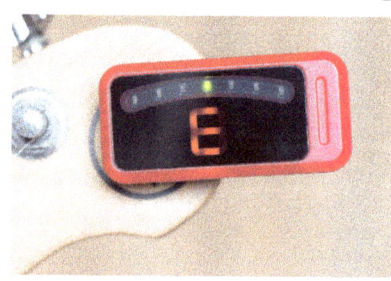

These two pictures show what an electronic tuner looks like and how it looks attached to the headstock. This type is great because it has a large display to see what the strings are tuned to. Remember, from the thickest string to the smallest, the tuning will be **E, A, D, G, B, and E**.

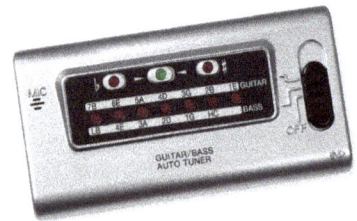 This tuner is a bit different, but works the same way. As you tighten or loosen the stings, an indicator light lets you know if you're in tune or not. These are great too they just don't clip on your headstock.

These types of tuners are not too difficult to figure out. That is why they are so popular. I suggest you get one, and learn to use it to keep your guitar in tune.

Lesson 4: Using a guitar pick

Now that we have the guitar in tune, we come to the next tool of the trade. Our infamous guitar pick. This little device will allow us to create a more pronounced sound when striking the strings.

Here are some samples of guitar picks:

Guitar picks come in different colors, textures, and sizes. It is best to try a few out to see what kind works best for you.

Once you decide on the type of pick that you like, you want to learn how to hold it. This will be looked at in further detail on the next page.

Learning to play the guitar is fun because it becomes a very personal journey. You can make it your own.

As you head down this journey, you'll discover things about yourself that you didn't know existed, and that's what makes it cool.

Make sure to take time to find the right guitar pick. This little tool can make a huge difference in your playing.

Like I said before, once we find the perfect pick, we need to learn to hold it properly. The two pictures below will help to teach us how to do this.

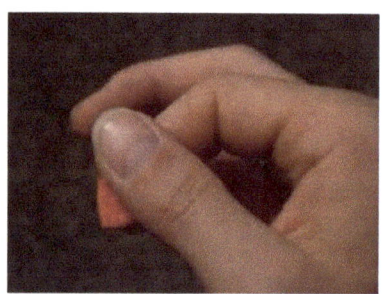

The thumb is placed over the top with your index finger bent underneath and the pointy end sticking out. See the picture to the left for reference.

The picture to the right shows the pick in a little more detail. Notice how the pick is being held in playing position.

The hand is close to the strings and the pick is ready to pick the strings individually, or to strum them altogether.

The guitar pick can be very beneficial in many ways.

- Helps to produce a clearly defined tone.
- Increases the overall volume.
- Helps with strumming chords.
- Helps to increase the speed of single-note melodies.

All this and more can be accomplished using a guitar pick, so don't overlook this lesson.

Summary
Chapter 2

In Chapter 2, we learned about two very important fundamental principles of playing the electric guitar. Tuning it and using a guitar pick. This will set up our foundation.

We first look at tuning the guitar. To do this correctly, we need to know the names of the strings, which we learned in lesson 3. Remember, you have 6 strings and 6 numbers, and the biggest number is the thickest string, and the smallest number is the thinnest string.

We then learn about the clip-on tuner, which is a great device for tuning the guitar. It's small and portable, clips nicely onto the headstock, and has a big display so we can easily see the string name we are tuning.

We then learn about another cool device called the guitar pick. This device helps you to get a more pronounced sound when strumming across the strings. We also learn that there are different ones to choose from, and it is held between the thumb and first finger.

We also learned that using a pick has many advantages. It helps to produce a clear defined tone, strumming chords, increase volume, and increase overall speed. There are even more benefits to using a guitar pick, so don't overlook this ingenious little tool.

Chapter 3

The Guitar Amplifier

Lesson 5: Role of the amplifier

What's different about the electric guitar from the acoustic guitar is the way it produces sound from the vibration of the strings. The acoustic uses a soundhole, as the electric uses magnets called pickups.

Amplifier example:

This guitar amplifier is a great invention in itself. It amplifies the string vibration that comes through the pickups. This allows you to control the volume of the electric guitar. Which is the reason it was invented in the first place.

Playing the acoustic guitar by itself could be heard fine, but when it was played with other instruments like drums and horns, it couldn't be heard very well. So, to fix the problem, the electric guitar was invented. To control the volume, the amplifier was needed.

How to set up your sound:

- **Electric guitar:**

There are many different types of electric guitars to choose from. I suggest you do some research and find one you like. Try your local music store. Even though you don't know how to play it yet, see how it feels in your hands.

- **Guitar cable:**

Once you find the guitar you like, you'll need a guitar cable to connect the guitar to the amplifier. This carries the signal of the vibrated strings to the amp and coms out the speaker.

- **Guitar amplifier:**

Although the sound comes out of the speaker, it is the amplifier that allows you to control the volume and tone of the signal. Make sure to research this as well. The right amplifier can make a world of difference in your overall tone.

Lesson 6: Getting the right tone:

- **Guitar, cable and amp:**

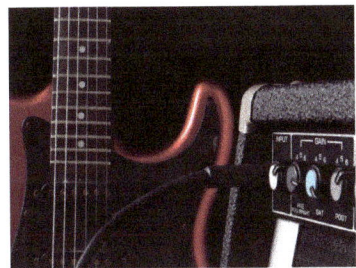

This is where you put these three tools together to create the ultimate combination of sound. Since everyone like different types of music, the guitar and amp combo will be different. But get this right, and you'll play guitar for years.

As you can see from the image to the right, the amplifier has a bunch of knobs on it. These knobs allow you to not only control the volume but also shape the tone.

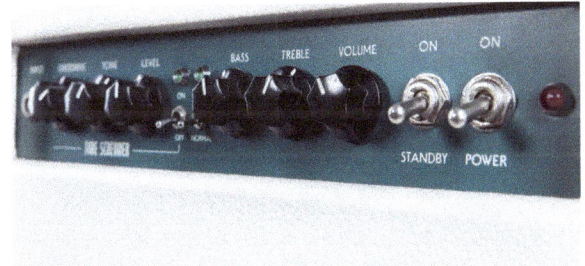

This is what makes the electric guitar so fun. You get to create a unique sound of your own, as well as get the sound of your favorite players. Nowadays, they have modeling amps that have great tones preset into them so it makes it even easier to get a great guitar tone.

Getting a good tone is highly important when it comes to playing the electric guitar. Be sure to take time to work on this so you can get the tone that works with the style of music you want to play with your guitar.

Gain, volume & treble

In this picture we have the gain, volume and treble knobs. The gain breaks up the signal to make it distort, great for rock. The treble cotrols the top part of the signal, allowing for a bright tone, and of course the volume knob allows to control signal strength.

Volume, bass & treble

This picture is similar except is shows a bass knob. This controls the bottom part of the signal. By controlling both the top and bottom with the treble and bass knobs, we can get a wide variety of textures out of the guitar amplifier.

Preamp, & cable

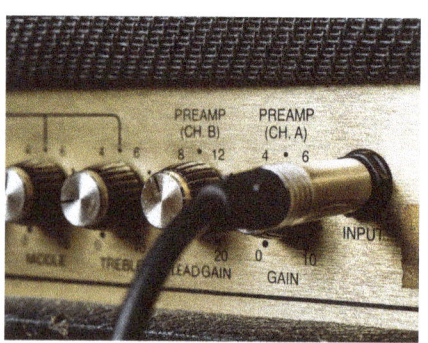

When the vibrational strings signal comes from your guitar to the amp, it is weak. The preamp allows this signal to be boosted so that it can be heard and shaped to the desire you choose. The guitar cable is plugged into the input of the amp for the signal to be received, and manipulated.

Summary
Chapter 3

In Chapter 3, we learn about the guitar amplifier. It is this specific item that allows us to increase the volume of the instrument. Not only that, but it also allows us to control the tone of the guitar.

To use the guitar amplifier, we need to add one more element, the guitar cable. This will allow us to connect the guitar to the amplifier. So, in setting up our sound, we have the guitar, cable, and amplifier.

Once you get your sound set up, you want to work on getting a good guitar tone. This is one thing that is different about the electric guitar than the acoustic. With the amplifier, you can shape your sound and add texture to it with the knobs of the amplifier.

This right here is a lot of the fun of playing the electric guitar. You get to create a sound that is all your own. As well as create sounds from your favorite players. This is all done through the knobs in the amplifier. To do this correctly, you will need to experiment.

The gain and the preamp knobs allow you to break up the signal and make it distort. The treble and bass knobs allow you to control the high and low frequencies, and all this allows you to get the tone you desire.

Chapter 4

Electric Guitar Chords

Lesson 7: Natural chords

The most common chords to play on the electric guitar are called natural chords. These are basic fundamental chords played around the first few frets. The best way to learn these is by reading chord charts.

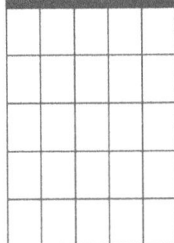

A chord chart is a diagram that shows a quick visual representation of the fretboard facing upward. It shows the 6 strings from left to right and the first 5 frets. It also shows you where to place your fingers when forming a guitar chord.

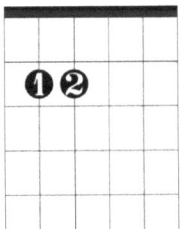

To the left, we have what is called an **E minor chord**. The chart shows two dots on the 5th and 4th strings on the 2nd fret. The numbers indicate which fingers to use when forming this chord.

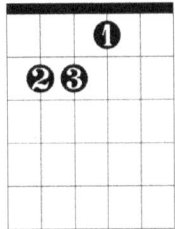

This chord chart shows the **E major chord**. As you can see, it is the same except we add a finger to the 3rd string 1st fret. We also need to change fingers as we now will be using our third finger also.

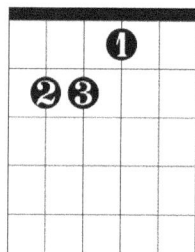

This is the **A minor chord**. If you look at this chord, it is the same shape as the E major, just a string down. This makes it an easy transition from the E minor and E major chords.

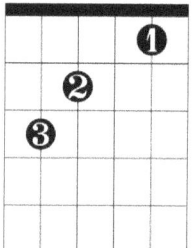

This is the **C major chord**. One of the most common chords you'll come across in songs. It is an easy transition from A minor, as you only need to move one finger. Also, look how easy it would be to transition to E minor.

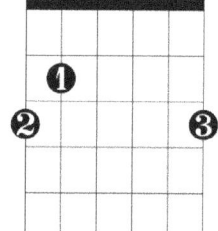

This is the **G major chor**d. Another very common chord that is in many popular songs. This one is a bit tricky to form because it stretches across all 6 strings. This chord goes great with C major.

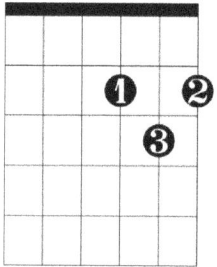

This is the D major chord. Formed on the 1st, 2nd, and 3rd strings on the 2nd and 3rd frets. There are many chords, but these are the most common, found in hundreds of songs. Work on forming and switching between them.

**When forming these chords, work at playing on your fingertips.

Lesson 8: Power chords

Natural chords are played around the first few frets. To move up the fretboard, we need to play different types of chords. The type that is the easiest is the power chord. A two-note chord that spans 2 frets and is played with just two fingers.

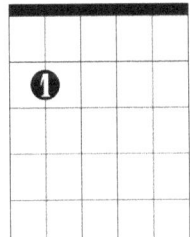

This chord is the **open E**. Since we have the string nut, this chord can be played with just one finger. It is called open E because the E string is not fretted. When this happens, it's called open.

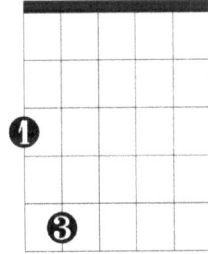

This is the root 6 G power chord. The reason why it's called a root 6 is that the G note (the chord root) is on the 6th string at the 3rd fret.

Power chords are very common in playing a lot of rock songs because when you put a little gain on them, they sound really cool. Remember what we discussed about gain in the last lesson?

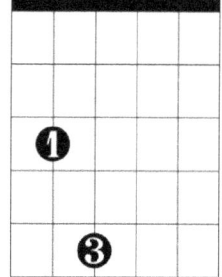

Can you see how this chord shape is the same as the G power chord? Two fingers on 2 strings, spanning 2 frets. This is the **Root 5 C power chord**. Why? Because the C note (the root of the chord) is on the 5th string.

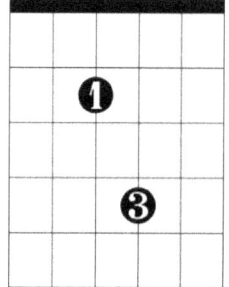

This is a **Root 4 E power chord**. Since there are only two notes, these are neither major nor minor. I'll explain about that later. Just work at forming the chords.

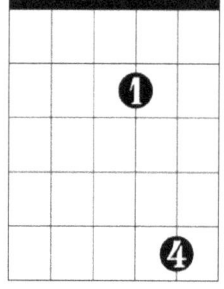

When it comes to playing a Root 3 power chord, we need to move one finger over a fret. This is because of the B string. Since it is different from the others, the notes line up differently. So here, you will need to span 3 frets. This is the **Root 3 A power chord.**

Power chords are how you play along the fretboard. They stay the same shape when you play them, unlike the natural chords. Work at forming them and moving them up and down the fretboard. They'll come in real handy when you start learning to play songs.

Tritone Publishing © 2025

Summary
Chapter 4

In Chapter 4, we learned about electric guitar chords. The two most common are natural chords and power chords. Natural chords are chords that are played around the first few frets. The best way to read these is by reading chord charts.

Chord charts are diagrams that show a quick visual representation of the fretboard facing upward. It shows the 6 strings from left to right and the first 5 frets. It also shows you where to place your fingers when forming a guitar chord.

These are very beneficial when it comes to reading the shapes of guitar chords. No matter if they are major chords, minor chords, power chords, or any other type of chord.

We then look at power chords. These are chord types that allow you to move up the fretboard. They are played with just two fingers, on two strings, with a fret in between them.

Later in the training, you will see how beneficial these are. For now, work on forming them and moving them around the fretboard. Both chord types will allow you to get a lot out of the guitar if you take the time to master them.

Play on your fingertips for the natural chords, and stretch your fingers out for the power chords.

Tritone Publishing © 2025

Chapter 5
Creating Rhythm

Lesson 9: Strumming chords

The most common way to play the chords that you previously learned is by strumming them. This is where you sweep the pick up and down across all 6 strings. This is how you create rhythm.

In this lesson, we'll explore some basic strumming patterns that will get you started and make your chords sound like music.

Strumming pattern #1: Strum down.

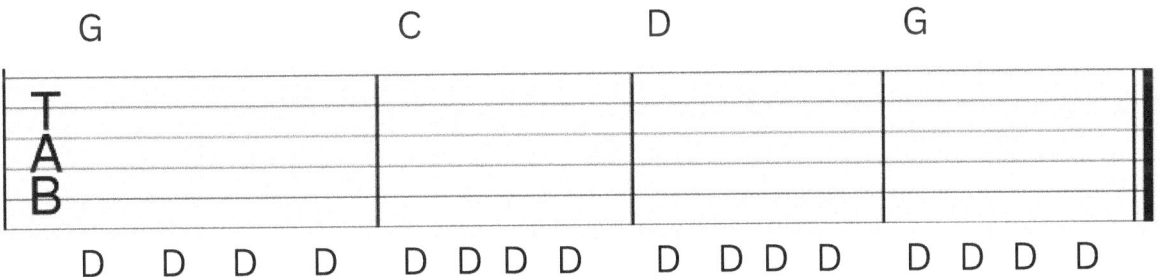

In this first example, you use 3 chords: Many songs are made up of only 3 chords. Strum downward across all six strings 4 times on each chord.

Make sure to keep a slow, steady tempo while strumming downward. This might seem a bit awkward at first, but don't worry, it will get smoother over time.

Tritone Publishing © 2025

Strumming pattern #2: Down & back up.

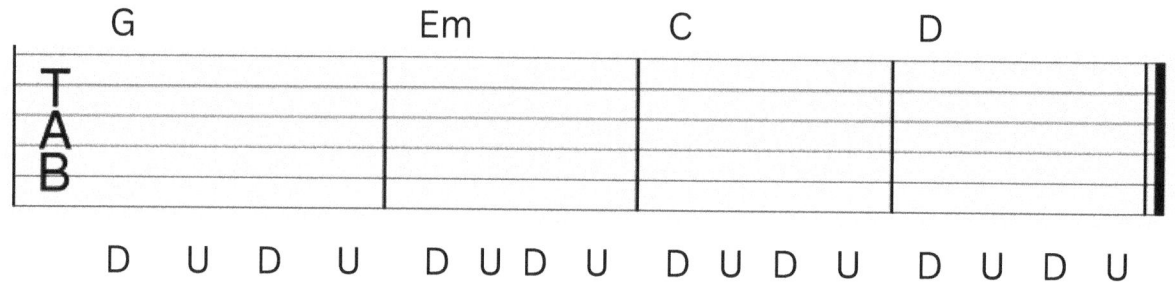

In this 2nd example, you strum down and then back up. As you do this, you will develop better coordination in your picking hand.

Strumming pattern #3: Down-up-down.

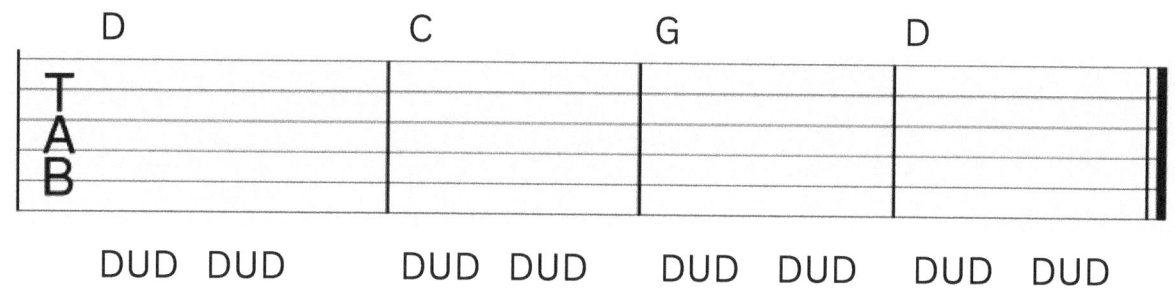

In this 3rd example, you strum three beats together as one. Make sure to keep it slow and steady. Speed will come with practice. Notice how this creates a different type of rhythm.

Lesson 10: Developing proper timing

When you create rhythm, it is not enough to just strum chords, you want to do it in such a way that it sounds like music. This is where proper timing comes in. This is developed with timing sequences.

Timing sequence #1: quarter note

Timing sequence #2: Eight note

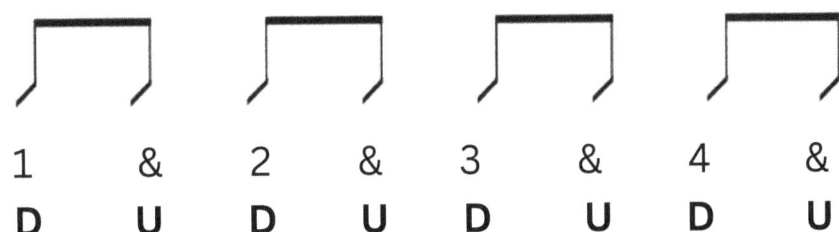

In these examples, we use quarter and eighth notes to establish proper timing. This is similar to the last lesson, but this time, we count as we strum. I can't emphasize enough the importance of counting. Do not overlook this.

In these next two examples, we are going to combine them to create rhythm patterns that are even more interesting.

Timing sequence #3: 2 quarter & 2 eighth

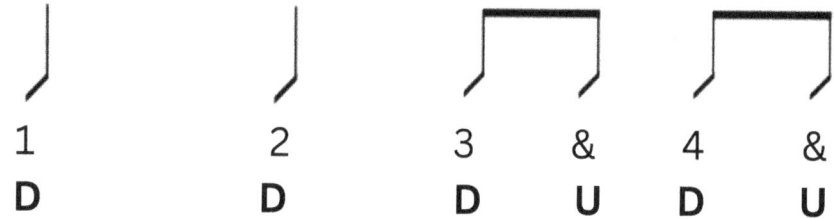

1	2	3	&	4	&
D	**D**	**D**	**U**	**D**	**U**

Timing sequence #4: 1 quarter & 3 eighth

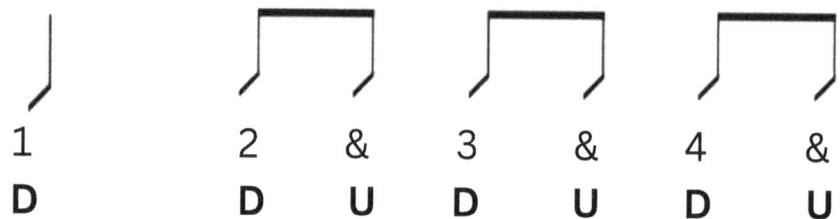

1	2	&	3	&	4	&
D	**D**	**U**	**D**	**U**	**D**	**U**

Can you see how this simple concept creates different rhythm patterns while you strum chords? If you work at it enough, you'll soon come up with even more interesting rhythms.

Summary
Chapter 5

In Chapter 5, we learned about how to create rhythm. We will do this by strumming chords and developing proper timing. This will develop our picking hand and bring the chords that we've learned to life.

First, we look at strumming chords. This is where you sweep the pick across the strings to create music and is done with an up-and-down motion.

We explore 3 common strumming patterns. Strumming downward. Strum across all six strings 4 times per chord. We then look at strumming down and back up again. Finally, we look at combining these two techniques.

In lesson 10, we learn that when you create rhythm, it is not enough to just strum chords; you want to do it in such a way that it sounds like music. This is where proper timing comes in. This is developed with timing sequences.

We then look at how we can use quarter notes and eighth notes to create different rhythms. You must master counting. I know it sounds easy, but in reality, it isn't. You'd be amazed how many people skip this step.

Remember, it's not enough to know the chords and the motion of strumming, you must be able to do it with proper timing.

Chapter 6
Reading Guitar Tabs

Lesson 11: Chords

In addition to reading chord charts, it is a good idea to learn to read guitar tabs.   These are similar, except the 6 lines representing the strings will be horizontal instead of vertical.

These are more useful than charts because we can use them for both chords and melody lines. Let's see how we can first use them for reading chords.

Gutar tab example #1: Guitar tab measure

Here, we have a guitar tab measure. As you can see, we have 6 horizontal lines that represent the strings. Numbers will be placed on these lines to indicate frets. The thing you've got to remember with guitar tabs is that your biggest string (6th string) is on the bottom. Opposite of your guitar.

Here are the chords previously learned written in guitar tabs.

E minor

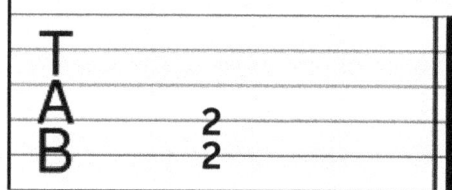

E major

A minor

C major

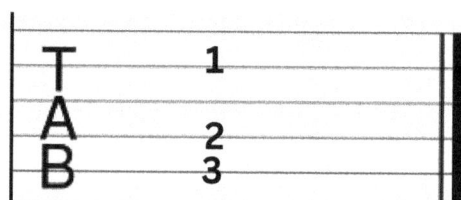

G major

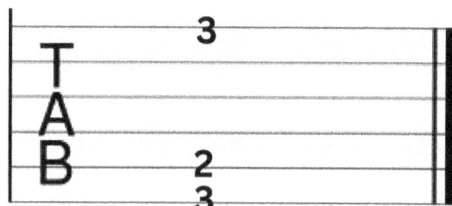

D major

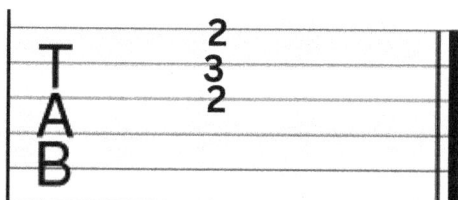

Lesson 12: Melody

Like I said, in addition to reading chords in guitar tab format, we can also use it for single note melodies. These are where we play the notes individually one right after the other. These can be on one string or multiple strings.

This allows us to venture further up the fretboard for more creative musical pieces. We add these to our guitar chords, and we enhance the way we can approach the instrument.

Here are a few examples:

Practice slowly:

Here, we play the 5th fret and the 7th fret. One right after another. Both are on the same string.   When we strum chords, the notes are stacked and played together. Single notes will be side by side.

Example #1: All notes played on the 6th string

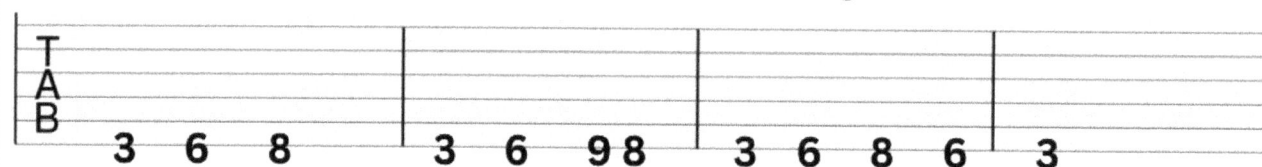

In this first example, all notes are on the 6th string. Remember, the 6th string is on the bottom, and focus on timing.

Example #2: All notes played on the 5th string

In this second example, all notes are on the 5th string. Very similar to the first example, except different frets on a different string.

Example #3 All notes played on the 4th, 5th, & 6th strings

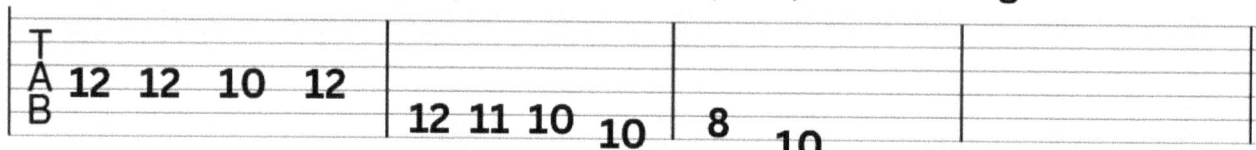

In this last example, notes are played on multiple strings, and it gives you a chance to play further up the fretboard. Start on the 4th string and proceed to the 6th string.

Summary
Chapter 6

In Chapter 6, we learned about reading guitar tabs. These are similar to chord charts we previously learned. The difference is that the lines that represent the guitar strings are horizontal instead of vertical. Also, the 6th string is on the bottom.

These are more useful because they allow us to indicate further up the fretboard with not only chords but with melody lines. Also, with guitar tabs, we use numbers to indicate the frets we place our fingers on. This makes it a nice visual of the fretboard.

In addition to reading chords in guitar tab format, we can also use it for single note melodies. These are where we play the notes individually one right after the other. These can be on one string or multiple strings.

This allows us to venture further up the fretboard for more creative musical pieces. We add these to our guitar chords, and we enhance the way we can approach the instrument. Go through the examples in the lesson and see how melody lines sound.

Remember, the hardest part of our guitar-playing journey is at the start. This is where the most work is necessary. Developing the proper skills to sound great on the instrument. Do this properly, and these skills will last us a lifetime.

Tritone Publishing © 2025

Chapter 7
Guitar Riffs

Lesson 13: Harmony riffs

What's cool about playing guitar is guitar riffs. These are small bits of music that are easily recognizable. We can do it with harmony (chords) and melody (single notes) as well. In this lesson, we'll look at harmony guitar riffs that will make people say, "Wow, that's cool"!

Harmony Riff #1:

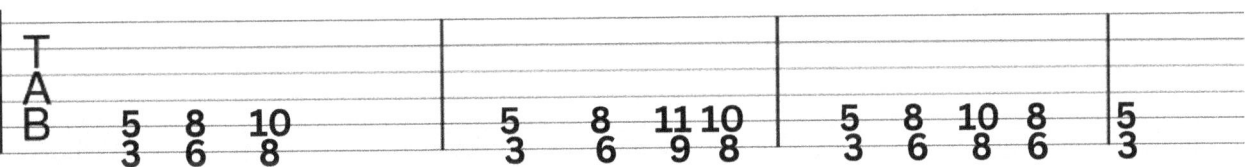

A harmony riff is when you play a guitar riff with chords. Here is an example with power chords on the 6th string.

Harmony Riff #2:

In this example, we play chords on two different strings. On the 5th and the 6th strings. This gives us an opportunity to move around the fretboard on different strings.

Harmony Riff #3:

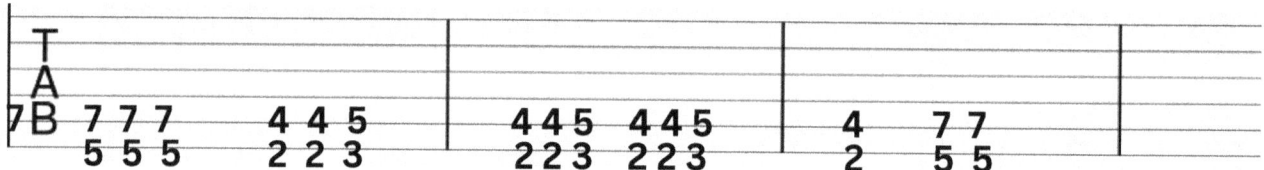

In this third riff, we stay on the 6th string but play the riff in a sequence of three. This will help to improve our timing when we create rhythms.

Harmony Riff #4:

In this last riff, we use open chords and a single note. Remember the open E power chord? Well, if you bring it down a string, it becomes an open A chord. Move down a string more, it becomes an open D chord.

All these harmony riffs will help to get familiar with the fretboard as well as improve the skill of creating rhythms. Power chords are very popular in playing electric guitar, and this will allow you an opportunity to master them for future reference.

Lesson 14: Melody riffs

The other type of riffs we want to master are single-note melody riffs. These are very beneficial in developing finger independence. Not to mention ear training.

Melody Riff #1:

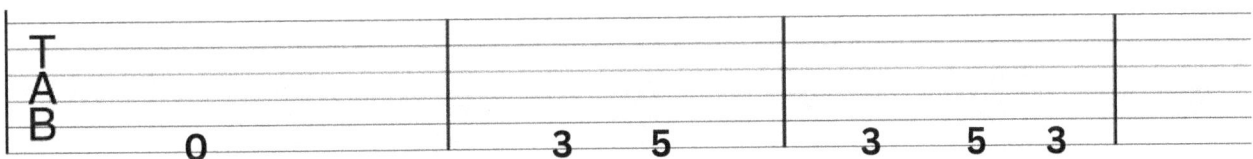

This chord is a bit odd as well, but it is found in many popular songs. and they also do things as

Melody Riff #2:

This chord is a bit odd as well, but it is found in many popular songs. and they also do things as

Melody Riff #3:

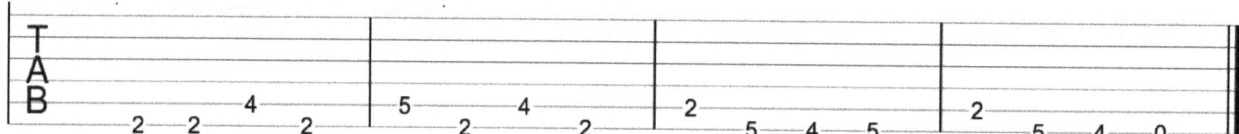

In melody riff #3, we stretch out a bit. Although we only play on the 5th and 6th strings, we need to stretch out to the 4th and 5th frets. This will be another great exercise for building finger strength and dexterity.

Melody Riff #4:

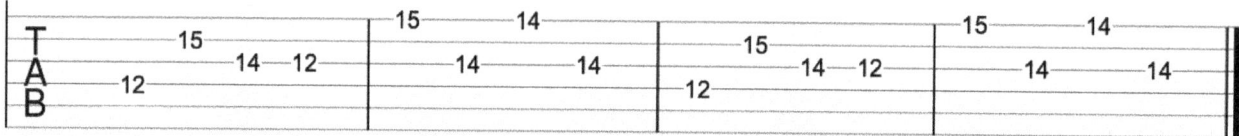

In this last melody riff, we get to challenge ourselves. Are you up for it? This one is played further up the fretboard and skips strings. Once again, a great exercise for building finger independance.

Both of these lest two riffs can be challenging. But, if you get them down, it will excel your guitar playing.

Playing melody of any kind is a great way to express yourself with the electric guitar. We will look at this approach more in the next lesson on intro to lead guitar. For now, just make sure you can execute these.

Summary
Chapter 7

In Chapter 7, we learned about guitar riffs. These are small bits of music that are easily recognizable. We can do it with harmony (chords) and melody (single notes) as well. In this lesson, we'll look at harmony guitar riffs that will make people say, "Wow, that's cool"!

Harmony riffs will help you get familiar with the fretboard as well as improve your skill in creating rhythms. Power chords are very popular in playing electric guitar, and this will allow you an opportunity to master them for future reference.

The examples in the lesson will allow you to work on your power chords. On both the 5th and 6th strings. As well as develop your open power chords. All these examples will help you to master the fretboard.

In the next lesson, we look at single-note melody riffs. These help you out with finger independence and ear training. These are both two fundamental principles that are beneficial to develop.

The last two examples are a bit tricky, but they help to develop finger strength because they expand your finger stretch. If you work on these daily, you'll see some great improvement in your guitar playing.

Harmony and melody guitar riffs are a great way to read guitar tabs as well as approach the guitar in multiple ways.

Tritone Publishing © 2025

Chapter 8

Into To Lead Guitar

Lesson 15: Major & minor pentatonic

Now, we come to one of my favorite chapters. Playing lead guitar. The best way to get started is with the pentatonic scale. A scale of five notes that works wonders in this area.

Penta means 5, and tonic means tones or notes. A scale of 5 notes. Since there are 5 notes, we can create 5 scale patterns, which work great for playing in both major and minor keys.

Now, I don't want to get too technical about these, as this is just an introductory lesson, but we will learn how they look across the fretboard and how to make music with them.

The one that is the most popular is the minor pentatonic scale. This is because of the way it is shaped and the ease of playing it.

The A minor Pentatonic Scale:

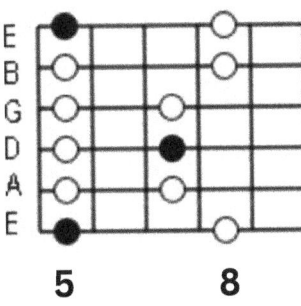

Here is the minor pentatonic scale in A at the 5th fret. It spans across all 6 strings and forms a box pattern. Start with your index finger at the 5th fret and proceed forward through the scale.

The C major Pentatonic Scale:

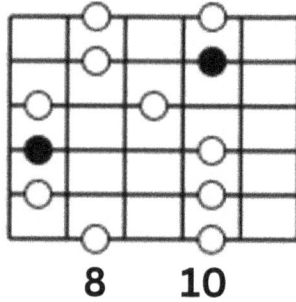

8   10

This is the C major pentatonic scale because it starts at the C note at the 8th fret. If we played it at the 3rd fret, it would be the G major pentatonic scale.. Notice how the pattern is different.

There are five box patterns, and they connect like puzzle pieces. Each one starts where the previous one left off. This allows you to span the whole fretboard and stay in key while playing lead guitar.

Additional pentatonic scale patterns

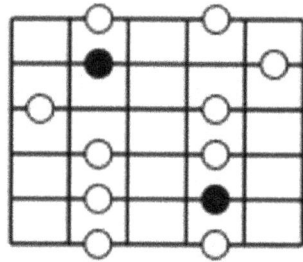 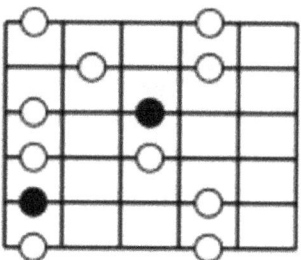 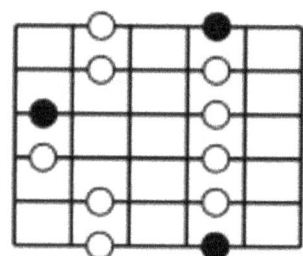

These five scale box patterns are just variations of the same five notes. But what's cool about them is they all represent a different type of character. I suggest you go through them and make the discovery..

Lesson 16: Lead guitar phrasing

Now that we know how to play the pentatonic scales, we can look at ways to make them sound musical. This is called lead guitar phrasing.

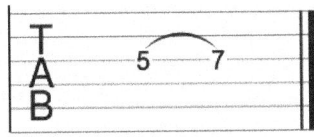
Hammer-on: This is where you pick a note and hammer-on to the next one after without picking the second note.

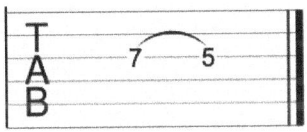
Pull-off: This is the same thing but in reverse. Two fingers down, you pick the note and pull-off to the one behind it.

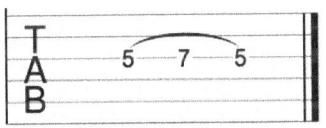
Hammer-on, pull-off: This is where you use the two techniques together across three notes. You hammer-on and then pull-off.

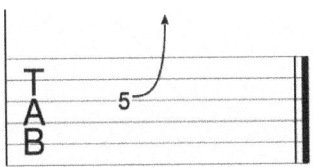
String bend: Here, you pick a note and slightly bend it up. I know the tab looks like you're going down, but just bend upward.

Vibrato: Here, you pick a note and slightly bend it up and down to create a vibrating effect.

All these are common techniques in playing lead guitar. So be sure to master them.

Phrasing exercise #1:

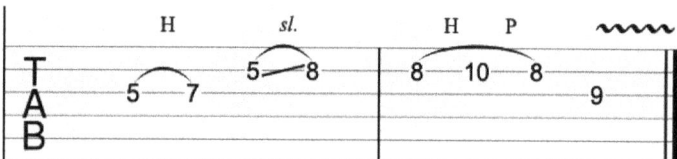

This first phrase uses a hammer-on, slide, hammer-on pull-off, and ends with a vibrato.

Phrasing exercise #2:

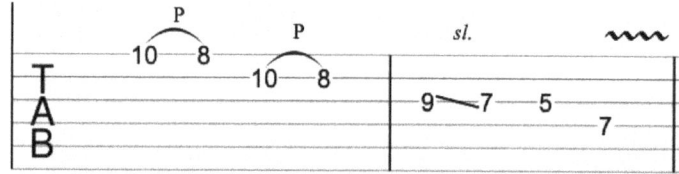

This second phrase uses two pull-offs, a slide down and a vibrato at the end.

Phrasing exercise #3:

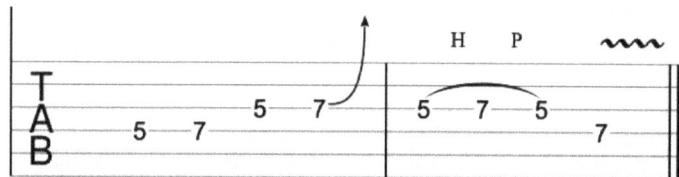

This third phrase uses a bend, a hammer-on pull-off and ends with a vibrato. Remember, vibrato is a great way to end a phrase.

Practicing this chapter daily will benefit your guitar plying in many ways. Ear training, note intervals, finger dexterity, rhythm, and timing.

Summary
Chapter 8

In Chapter 8, we learn about playing lead guitar. This is another very popular approach to playing the guitar. This is where you will use scales instead of chords. The best scales to start with are the pentatonic scales.

The pentatonic scale is a scale of 5 notes. Penta means 5, and tonic means tones or notes. A scale of 5 notes. Since there are 5 notes, we can create 5 scale patterns, which work great for playing in both major and minor keys.

The minor pentatonic scale is the first one to start with because it is the easiest to play. I recommend you learn all 5 that are presented in the lesson. This will allow you to move throughout the fretboard as well as master the different box patterns.

The next thing we learn is how to use these scales to create music. This is called phrasing.   Phrasing to guitar players is like writing is to novelists. You learn things such as hammer-ons, pull-offs, slides, bends, etc, and use them to create music.

If you learn the techniques mentioned above and practice the phasing examples presented in the lesson, you'll have a leg up if you decide to further your education in this area. Remember, lead guitar playing takes dedication and practice.

Tritone Publishing © 2025

Chapter 9
Basic Music Theory

Lesson 17: Notes on the fretboard

When it comes to learning music theory, it starts with the 12 notes of the musical alphabet. A-G#. This is also called the chromatic scale. This means, that all the notes reside right next to each other.

Music alphabet: A A# B C C# D D# E F F# G G#

If you notice, all the notes have a # after them except for two. The B and the E. Remember this. All 12 notes will reside on each string.

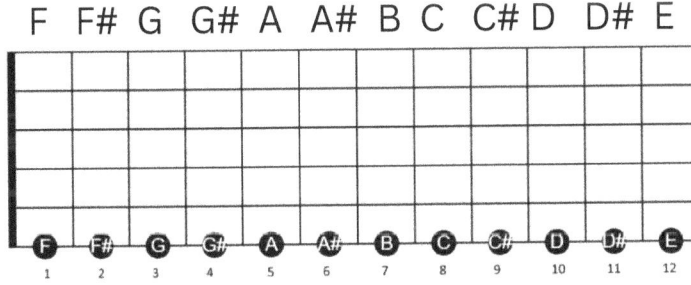

The **Low E string**. The string by itself will be the E note, and then it will proceed from there. Notes will repeat after the 12th fret.

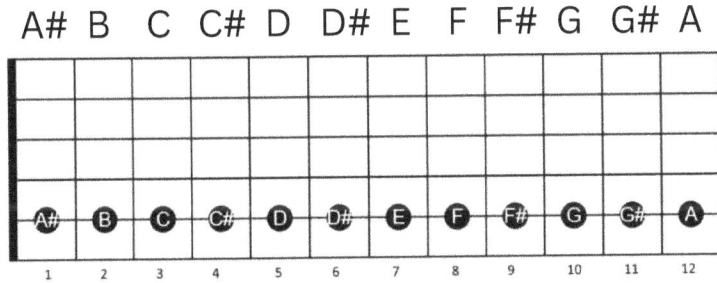

The A **string**. The string by itself will be the A note, and then it will proceed from there. Notes will repeat after the 12th fret.

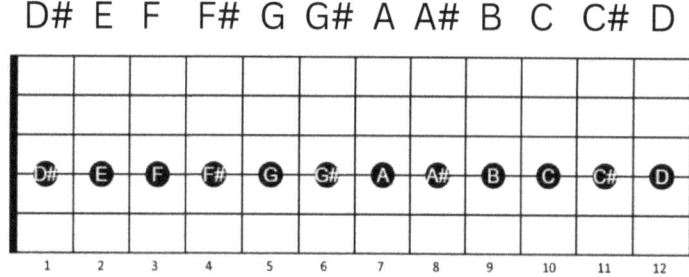

The D string. The string by itself will be the D note, and then it will proceed from there. Notes will repeat after the 12th fret.

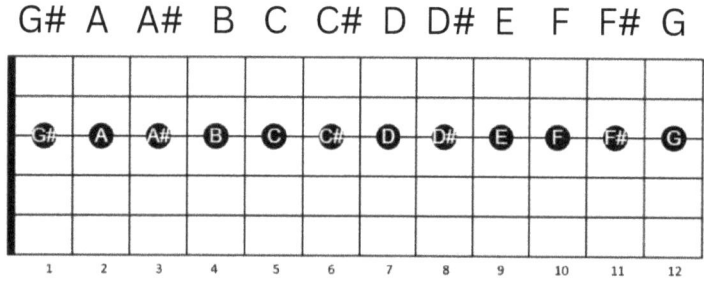

The G string. The string by itself will be the G note, and then it will proceed from there. Notes will repeat after the 12th fret.

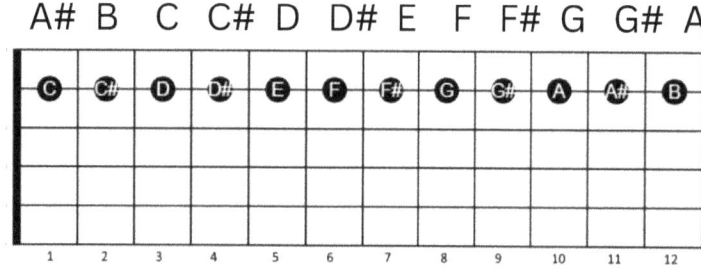

The B string. The string by itself will be the B note, and then it will proceed from there. Notes will repeat after the 12th fret.

** I didn't add the high E string because the notes are the same as the notes on the low E string.

Tritone Publishing © 2025

Lesson 18: Chord & scale theory

In the previous lesson, I showed you all the notes on the fretboard. I recommend you go through these daily until you memorize them. They will come in handy for this lesson on chord construction. As well as any other lesson you might study further down the line on music theory.

Out of the 12 notes of the music alphabet, we take 7 to create the major scale. This major scale will be the foundation for all chords and other scales you might learn in the future.

Here is an example:

C major: C D E F G A B. These particular notes are chosen because the scale must have the Do Re Mi sound for it to be diatonically correct. All major scale notes in all keys will be chosen because of this concept.

Now that we know the notes, we can give each one a number value.

C D E F G A B
1 2 3 4 5 6 7

It is these 7 notes in the C major scale, that the C major chord will be created out of. All chords have a note formula that comes from the notes of the key they come out of.

All chords learned so far can be created from the notes of the keys they come out of. The keys of A major, B major, C major, D major, etc. These are created by using 3 notes. The 1, the 3, and the 5th notes.

A major: A B C# D E F# G#
          1 2 3 4 5 6 7

A major chord: 1 3 5.   **A minor chord**: 1 b3 5 **A7**: 1 3 5 b7
          A C# E   **A C E**   **A C# E G**

Can you see how these chords are created out of the notes within the key? In the case of the minor and the 7th chord, we flatten the 3rd and the 7th note. With this concept, we could create an Am7th, by adding the flat 7th note to the minor chord. This is the science of music.

C major: C D E F G A B   **A minor: A B C D E F G**
         1 2 3 4 5 6 7   1 2 b3 4 5 6 b7

C major pentatonic: 1 2 3 5 6 **A minor pentatonic: 1 b3 4 5 b7**
            C D E G A   **A C D E G**

See how this concept works the same way? If you check the notes of the scales you've learned so far, you'll see they are constructed from these notes. If you want to create chords or scales on the fly, you need to know your notes.

Summary
Chapter 9

In Chapter 9, we learn a little bit about music theory. This covers notes on the fretboard, and chord construction. When it comes to learning music theory, it all comes down to the 12 notes of the musical alphabet. Or sometimes called the chromatic scale.

These 12 notes will be A A# B C C# D D# E F F# G and G#. These are the notes that are in music styles like Jazz, Country, Blues, Pop, Rock, etc. They are also found on each of the 6 guitar strings. Knowing where these notes are on each string will allow us to create chords on the fly, by mastering the fretboard.

Lesson 17 goes through the notes on each string, and we learn that the notes always follow the same order. We just start on the note that the string is associated with. If it is the D string, we start with the D note and proceed from there.

Next, in lesson 18, we learn that we take 7 notes out of the 12 to create a key like C major. Out of these 7 notes, we can create chords like majors, minors, and the 7th chord. This is the science of music. Each chord has a specific note formula.

By learning about these note formulas and knowing the notes that are in specific keys, we can create a wide variety of chords and scales, not just the ones that we have learned.

Chapter 10
Additional Training

Lesson 19: Practice Habits

Practice habits are what you develop along your journey of learning to play the electric guitar. How well these habits are formed will be a determining factor on how you sound when you play it.

Do you want to become an average guitar player or an above-average guitar player? Well, your focus, discipline, and determination to daily practice will answer this question.

Not only can this help you with guitar playing, but it can also help you with other aspects of your life. Let's look at a few tips to help in this area of improvement.

- **Set A Guitar Goal:**

When you set a guitar goal, you have something to shoot for. You develop a purpose for why you're doing all the work. This will help you to stay focused and progress faster.

- **Track Your Progress:**

When you track your progress, you see clearly what areas you are doing well in and what areas you need to improve on. This will increase your chances to stay motivated and succeed.

- **Create A Practice Space:**

This is a place where you can focus on your studies. A place with no distractions. A spare bedroom, basement, garage, etc. Do this, and you will be well on your way to guitar greatness.

- **Get Yourself Organized:**

This is another key element on your journey. Getting organized will allow you to progress faster, reduce wasted time, stay focused longer, and boost your overall creativity.

- **Develop A Practice Routine:**

Since repetition is the key to succes, developing a practice routine can help you to get the most out of the time you have. With a daily planned structure of activities, you'll know exactly what to work on.

- **Consistent Daily Practice:**

This is the key to it all right here. Consistent Daily Practice! This is where most people fail. Make sure to follow this rule, and remember, nothing can be accomplished without consistency!

Lesson 20: Ear training

Reading notation is a great way to learn to play the guitar for all the reasons you've learned throughout this training. However, the most common way that people learn is by ear. This is where you can transfer what you hear to the fretboard without notation.

In this final lesson of the training, we will look at a few tips that can help you to develop this universal ability.   Now, the best way to do this is to have the guitar in your hand 12 hours a day. But unfortunately, we can't all do this. So, let's look at a few alternatives.

Tips For Ear Training Development:

- **Master The Major Scale:**

Everything revolves around the major scale. All chords and scales are created out of it. The better you know this, the better your foundation for ear training.

- **Focus On Note Intervals:**

An interval is the distance between notes. These ascend and descend the musical alphabet. Your goal is to be able to recognize them by listening and applying them to the fretboard.

- **Go Through Notes In Any Key:**

The best way to recognize note intervals is by going through them in all 12 keys. This will not only help you with that but also help you to master the fretboard.

- **Get Your Voice Involved:**

When you get your voice involved, it helps to train your ear. You play a note and then sing the rest within a scale. This helps with note interval recognition within chords and scales.

- **Learn To Play Simple Melodies::**

Learning to play simple melodies is a great way to train your ear. The reason for this is that you can usually hum them. This helps with the connection you want to make with the guitar.

- **Practice, Practice, Practice:**

The best way to train your ear is to practice, practice, practice. If you follow the suggestions laid out for you in this lesson, you will see results. But for this to happen, you must make an effort daily.

Summary
Chapter 10

In Chapter 10, we take a look at a couple more things that can help us to become great guitar players. Developing practice habits and training our ears to recognize notes.

Practice habits are what you develop along your journey of learning to play the electric guitar. How well these habits are formed will be a determining factor on how you sound when you play it.

Remember, your focus, discipline, and determination to daily practice will effect how good of a guitar player you become.

In addition to the practice habits we develop, we should take some time to develop ear training. This eliminates the need for looking at sheet music and is another popular way to approach playing the guitar.

Make sure to master the major scale. This is the foundation for all chords and scales. The better we can hear this, the better we'll be able to find the notes on the fretboard.

Also, work on all the other tips taught in lesson 20. All these things focused on and practiced daily can help to develop your ear to hear the notes and transfer them to the guitar. But they must be worked on daily to get the most out of them.

Electric Quiz

Assess your learning

All answers are within the lessons. Find them there if you don't know the question. Good luck.

Q: What are the parts of the electric guitar?

A: _____

Q: What position is the guitar recommended to be played?

A: _____

Q: What device do you use to tune the guitar?

A: _____

Q: What is the benefit of using a guitar pick?

A: _____

Q: What is the role of the amplifier?
A: _____

Quiz Con't

Q: What does it mean to get the right tone?

A: _____

Q: What are natural chords?

A: _____

Q: What are power chords?

A: _____

Q: What does it mean to strum chords?

A: _____

Q: What is developing proper timing?

A: _____

Remember, this is just an assesment for you to check your progress and see what you still need to work on.

Quiz Con't

Q: What are guitar tabs?

A: _____

Q: What makes guitar tabs different from chord charts?

A: _____

Q: What are harmony riffs?
A: _____

Q: What are melody riffs?

A: _____

Q: What is the pentatonic scale?
A: _____

Remember, if you don't know the answer, don't fret, just go to the lesson it's associated with and find it.

Quiz Con't

Q: What is a hammer-on?

A: _____

Q: What is a pull-off?

A: _____

Q: What is a hammer-on pull-off ?
A: _____

Q: What is vibrato?

A: _____

Q: What does lead guitar phrasing mean?
A: _____

Remember, writing is just as important as reading. It helps with memory retention and communication enhancement.

Quiz Con't

Q: What are the 12 notes of the music alphabet?

A: _____

Q: What is the note formula for a major chord?

A: _____

Q: What is the note formula for minor chords?
A: _____

Q: Why are having good pracitce habits important?

A: _____

Q: What does training your ear accomplish?

A: _____

The more time you put into knowing the answer to all these questions, the better you will be able to express yourself on the guitar.

Conclusion

Electric Guitar 101

If you have made it this far I want to congratulate you. You have learned quite a bit about how to get started playing the electric guitar. Now, since this is only a beginner course, we haven't touched on all things electric, but we have enough to get you up and running.

If you learned all the lessons taught here in this training course, you should know about the electric guitar, how to hold it, strum basic chords, create rhythm, and a whole lot more.

If you feel you like playing rhythm, I recommend you check out some of my other books on playing rhythm guitar. If you like playing lead guitar, I recommend you check out one of my books on that.

If you feel you'd like to explore chord theory more, I recommend you check out my book on that. Or, possibly, you'd like to add the acoustic guitar to your skillset?

Whatever it may be, my books will set you on a path to guitar-playing success. Of course, that will only be if you stay focused, determined, and practice daily. Good luck, and have fun!

Tritone Publishing © 2025

Reference Guide

common chords

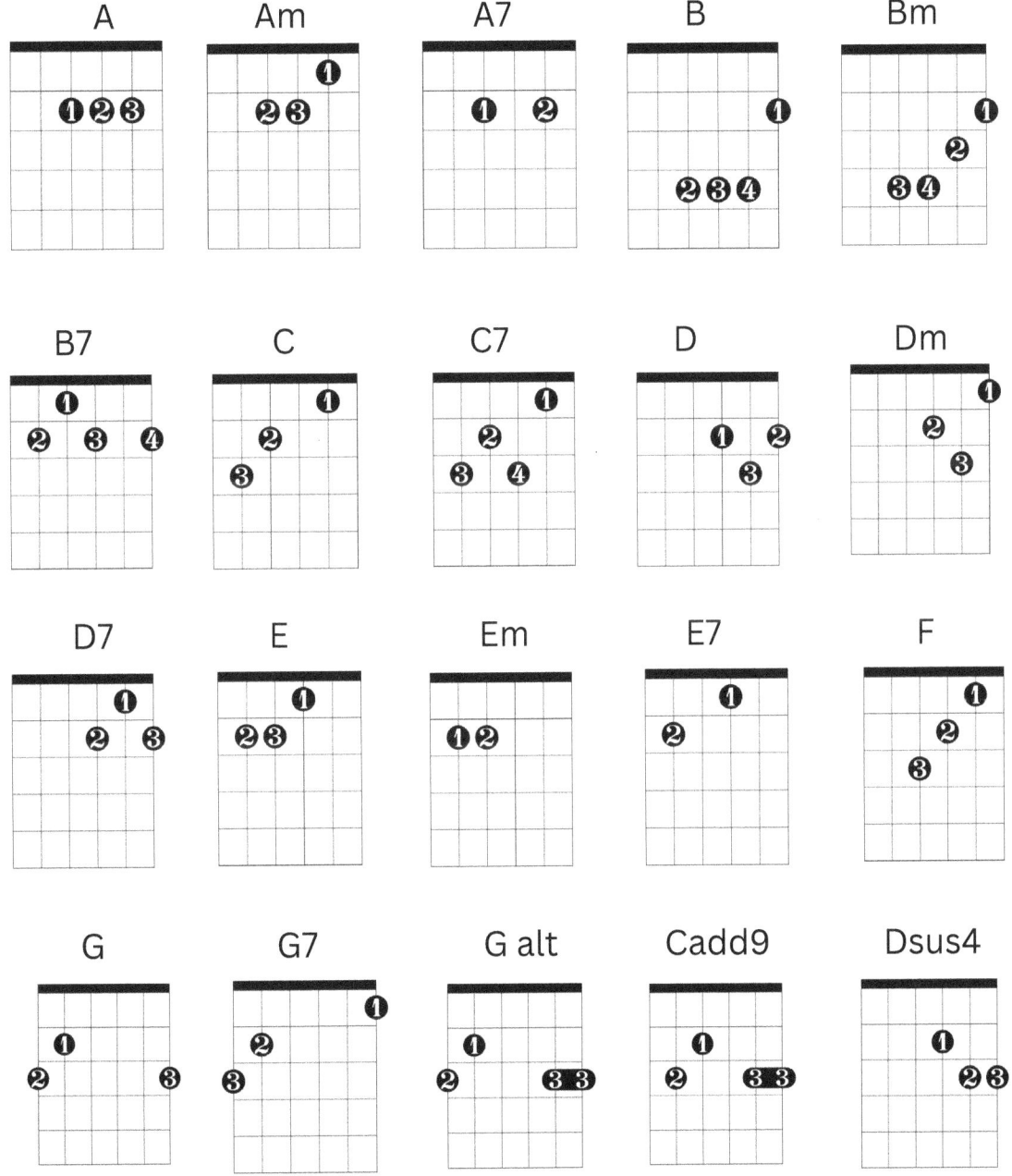

Tritone Publishing © 2025

Reference Guide

The 5 pentatonic scales

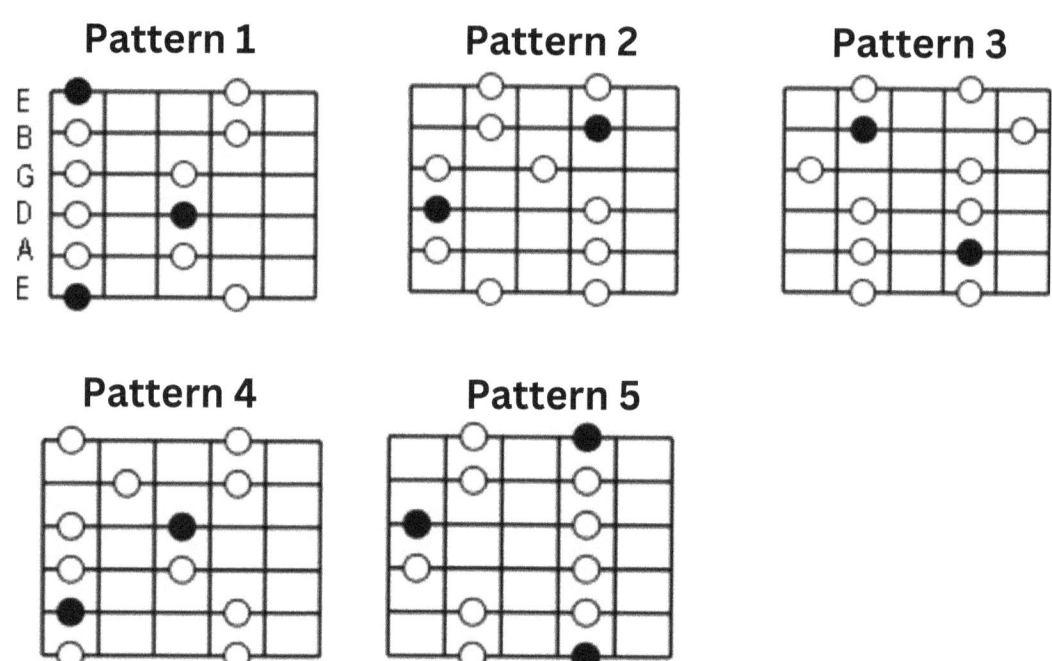

Pattern 1   Pattern 2   Pattern 3

Pattern 4   Pattern 5

Although there are many scales that can be played on the guitar, these 5 are the ones to get started with. These are very common im many guitar solos by great players.

If you have any questions about these contact me at my website, and also check out my Dwaynes Guitar Lessons YouTube Channel for free video lessons.

About The Author

DwaynesGuitarLessons.com

 Dwayne Jenkins is a professional guitar teacher, an accomplished musician, and an entrepreneur. He has been learning, playing, and teaching guitar lessons throughout Denver, CO, for over two decades.

He is now bringing his special training skills and methodology that have been honed and hand-crafted throughout the years on how to play to students around the world.

Dwayne has a unique, exciting approach that gets students of all ages and skill levels enjoying the fun of playing guitar and ukulele. His enthusiasm and love for teaching shine through every lesson that he creates.

His lessons are designed to enhance your ability to progress. No matter your reason for learning, there will always be something in Dwayne's books and products to help you achieve your dreams.

So, if you're a student looking to start or a student looking to further your education, be sure to get involved with Dwayne's guitar lessons. Either privately or through his books. You'll learn why playing the guitar is one of the greatest things you can do for yourself.

Tritone Publishing © 2025

Dive Deeper

Other Ttiles By Dwayne Jenkins

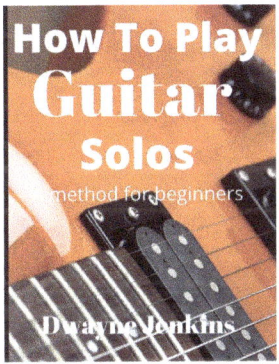

Al books can be found in paperback and digital format worldwide.

Tritone Publishing © 2025